AF223727

CORNELL N. WRIGHT

31 Coffee Breaks to a Better Organization

First published by Solomon's Books, LLC 2018

Copyright © 2018 by Cornell N. Wright

All rights reserved. No part of this publication may be reproduced, stored or transmitted in any form or by any means, electronic, mechanical, photocopying, recording, scanning, or otherwise without written permission from the publisher. It is illegal to copy this book, post it to a website, or distribute it by any other means without permission.

ISBN: 978-1-64370-134-9

For permission requests, write to author at the address below:

Cornell N. Wright

P.O. Box 261

Stratford, CT 06615-0261

www. solomonsbooks.org

Cover design by Cornell N. Wright

Edited by Solomon's Books

First edition

This book was professionally typeset on Reedsy.
Find out more at reedsy.com

Contents

Preface

<u>How to use Conversation Starters</u>

Welcome to a coffee break with a purpose!

Let's have a cup of coffee...and talk about your organization. The coffee break, as with any good cup of coffee, or tea, is best enjoyed when shared with someone else, especially with colleagues.

The 31 writings in this book are columns that were first published in the *New Haven Register*, New Haven, Connecticut. The word limitation of newspaper columns lend itself to short story-telling, quick analysis and direct recommendations. Also, the nature of business columns is non-serial that's why you can utilize the topics in this book in any sequence that suits your interest or business need.

The title of each conversation offers you a quick glimpse into the content of the original news column. The date that appears at the end of each conversation is the creation date which is close to the original publication time-frame.

So...as you read the offerings, over your favorite cup of coffee or tea, reflect on these real stories, the concepts and the recommendations. Share them with your colleagues and determine which concepts and stories might be of the greatest value to your organization.

As always, *Plan Well* and *Execute.*

Acknowledgement

I wish to thank Irene Jacqueline Wright, my late mother and friend, Joanne Parker Wright, my best friend and wife, Elaine Norton Jackson, my friend and personal editor and Mignon Quillings, my friend and publisher. Without their support and encouragement I cannot imagine producing this work. My deepest thanks to each of you. Also, thanks to the publisher and editors at the *New Haven Register* for their support and the opportunity to write columns for the newspaper.

1. Scenario Planning

In recent memory, we have not had as many significant natural occurrences in such a short period of time. The hurricanes that hit the greater Houston area, the Miami area, the Caribbean and especially the Puerto Rico area, the earthquakes in Mexico City and the wild fires in the Western parts of the United States have all occurred in the past two months.

I have friends who live in Houston, relatives who live in Miami and associates with family members in Puerto Rico, and all are concerned for their loved ones. My heart goes out to the citizens in Mexico City, too.

I mention these events for both business and personal reasons. When such events occur, we all stop for an instant and think about those who are directly impacted. Whether they are family and friends or business suppliers or customers, we pause.

I suggest that we take more than a pause and participate in scenario planning activities to provide us professionally and personally with a strategy to react to and to support those impacted by the disasters.

As a brief reminder, scenario planning activities are plans that are documented for some potential future occurrence that may or may not occur. A favorite scenario plan that most of us have created is the plan we would put in place if we won a major lottery prize. That same type of futuristic planning, to varying levels of detail, is the type of plan that should occur for natural disasters.

From the business side, let's take Miami as an example. Some questions that might need to be addressed would include: Status of our customers in the area? Are they capable of accepting our goods or services? Do they need more of our goods or services? How does their situation impact our business projections?

Questions abound on the suppliers' side as well. When will they be back in service? Do we have enough inventory for the next production cycle? Is there a critical product we need that is no longer available, like oranges, for example?

On the personal front, are our family and friends safe? If your daughter or son were in school in the area, what do you do? How can we get in touch with them? In my case, I could not contact my sister for four days. As a family, we'll work on a plan to help us stay in better touch in any future disaster.

My recommendation is that we take a few lessons from the recent disasters. We select a geographic area that has been known to have natural disasters. We then ask the scenario planning questions for that geography, for both business and personal planning. The solution for one geography will make the scenario plan easier for the next area that might impact you, your associates and your business. A world map in the planning room might be beneficial. An anonymous survey of your associates that will identify those geographies that are important to them will provide a list of the areas of concern to your team members.

Usually, we do not want to plan for negative occurrences. Hopefully the past two months are not an indicator of the future. Scenario planning can be beneficial either way.

   – October 1, 2017

2. Customer Service Plan

A customer service plan is an important element of your organization's overall planning and success.

Most organizations develop a marketing plan, or in some situations multiple marketing plans may be appropriate. The tried and true elements of, product, placement, promotion and price are the foundations of a solid marketing plan or marketing mix. However, the experiences of your customers are noticeably missing, as key elements of the typical marketing plan.

The rule of thumb is that it costs three to four times as much to gain a new customer as it does to maintain an existing customer. However, the underlying assumption is that the existing customer is pleased not only with the product, but pleased with your customer service as well.

I would offer that the price of a product or service is also heavily impacted by the associated customer service that accompanies the purchase. For example, in the event of a new television purchase, the initial customer service for the product might be the ease of operation and the quality of the instructions. I have a mental clock that starts when I open the box. If I beat the set-up and installation buzzer in my mind and the television is visually appealing, I have received good customer service and the cost is no longer an issue.

Additionally, as time goes on, when and if I refer back to the installation manual or I need to call customer technical service, the positive customer service involvement should continue. If it does, more than the price, promotion, or placement, the customer service will cause me to evaluate that brand first for the next television purchase.

I choose to look at the customer service's impact of a television. Many of us will be watching the Super Bowl today. Some will be watching the big game on televisions that are just short of unbelievable in size, technology and picture quality.

My point is that if customer service matters with a television purchase, how significant is customer service in other purchase decisions?

Functional products and services that deliver on their promises are critical to the success of any organization. Making your customers aware of your products is always important, especially in this product dense world. With the advent of internet shopping and timely deliveries for many products, placement does not carry the same significance as it once did. Price continues to be a decision factor; however, the pricing spectrum for most product categories continues to expand.

So, as you enjoy the game, consider how your organization's customer service impacts your customers' second and third purchases of your product and how improving your customer service plan can make that second purchase easier for your customers and more cost effective for you. – February 5, 2017

3. Roles, Alignment and Enthusiasm

I had the good fortune to view the University of Connecticut (UCONN) women play basketball this past weekend. My college basketball watching is not limited to them, but they have been the highlight of my viewing this season.

What I noticed in particular – not limited to the UCONN women but to all of the basketball teams – is the degree to which each player knows her or his role. By knowing their roles, I mean that each player on the team knows where to be on the court in any given circumstance whether on defense, offense or in transition. Additionally, the players cover for each other in the event that one has been bumped out of bounds; or a player has fallen or tried to make a steal and is momentarily out of position.

The players on the bench also have roles to play. They are watching their position to determine the best course of action against an individual opponent. Additionally, they are watching for strengths and weaknesses of the opponents' offense or defense. Most importantly, they are waiting for the coach to call their names to go into the game. This is when the attention prior to going into the game pays off, because they go into the game mentally prepared to assume their active role.

Even during the timeouts, the bench player's role is to encourage their teammates, make the huddle a safe place for the team and as quiet as possible. This is no easy feat because the home crowd is cheering and at away games the opposition is trying to be as disorienting as possible.

Our business organizations can learn a great deal about roles and preparation from your favorite basketball team. Three concepts come to mind among a long list of similarities. A top three could be alignment, roles and enthusiasm.

Alignment is the degree to which each member of the team, coaching staff, trainers, pep band cheerleaders, security and others knows the team's overall objective. In the case of the UConn women, this year's objective is to win an unprecedented fourth consecutive national title. All of the components of the organization are focused on that goal.

Roles are the positional work and contributions that each of the organization's components contribute to the alignment goals. At any one time, only five players are actively engaged in the pursuit of the objective. However, each of organization's components are skilled, practiced and functioning at a comparable level to the players on the court.

Enthusiasm is an amazing intangible benefit of most winning organizations. It does not take long to recognize the team or organization that has enthusiasm for its objective. The last of the three items might be the most important.

This week, take a look at your organization. If all of your organization's components are aligned to focus on the overall objective... great! If not, consider spending some time on creating more organizational alignment. Roles may be a little more difficult to evaluate. However, if you have experienced personnel growth or reduction you more than likely have some confusion in organizational roles.

Lastly, assess your organization's level of enthusiasm for the current plan, campaign or launch. You might be surprised. As the NCAA women's and men's basketball championships end this week notice the three elements and observe what you can bring back and adopt for your organization. – April 3, 2016

4. Management Assessment

I trust you enjoyed a Thanksgiving that included festive foods, football, family and or friends and a moment to recharge.

The celebration of Thanksgiving can offer a number of management lessons. Briefly, I will discuss one of the most important responsibilities of a manager — the identification of new managerial talent.

From my observations of families, volunteer kitchens and even the military during Thanksgiving festivities, there is usually one person in charge of the event. Let's call them the head chef. These managers of the events typically have held this responsibility for a number of seasons. As we know, seasons come to an end and the responsibilities have to be transferred to someone new.

The same holds true for organizations. There comes a time when new managerial talent has to be identified to continue the organization, allow for expansion, employee development or cross training. Every organization and manager evaluating potential new managers has a number of factors to consider. Those factors may be impacted by industry, growth stage, technology, demographics or other key decision-making criteria. In this space, I will only touch on four of those factors that I have found to be on most evaluation lists.

I have observed that managerial talent typically comes from someone who has performed well in their current position. The person may not be the number one performer but they usually ranked in the top 20 percent of performers. At the thanksgiving celebration, this person typically has stood by the head chef and performed assigned tasks in an admirable fashion. You can't mess up the recipes.

The person has to understand the culture of the family or organization. There is a place for new ideas, which partially account for the expansion of the menu. However, an appreciation of the history and tradition goes far in assuring that the head chef is comfortable that the baseline of the celebration continues.

Before someone is offered a managerial opportunity, he or she is usually given some type of test. The test in a Thanksgiving setting might be to prepare one or more elements of the dinner. In business, it might be a temporary assignment or project lead position. This delegation is also of value to the head chef. He or she has to be prepared to transfer their responsibilities to someone new.

Temperament is a vital element in the determination of managerial talent. The manner in which a person reacts under pressure or when things go sideways is critical. Also, the new manager will be the face of the organization and as such carries the reputation and image of your firm. Additionally, the team members who report to this person will be impacted positively or negatively by this managerial selection's temperament.

The wrong assessment of management talent will force you to make the decision again. A correct assessment will make your organization stronger, more capable to withstand the various demands of the marketplace, and you will be able to sleep more soundly at night.
   – November 27, 2016

5. Bird of Paradise and Bird of Prey

A decision to improve an organization's customer service is not a decision that should be arrived at lightly. The benefits associated with improved customer service fall into the large categories of increased sales, improved customer satisfaction and competitive advantage, to name just three.

Typically, the reasons for changing an organization's view toward customer service stem from an exposure to new information. A customer survey might have shown a weakness in the customer service area. Recurring competitive losses or a high-profile loss of a customer might provide the motivation for the change. Also, new members of the management team could usher in a course change toward improved customer service.

Regardless of the reasons for the change, the movement toward increased customer focus will require changes throughout the organization.

Allow me to make a distinction between lip-service and an actual focus on the customer. Nearly every organization will say that they are customer-focused. For many, that statement is true and misleading at the same time. In the lip-service organizations the customer focus is limited to identification, marketing and sales to the customer. Therefore, a customer focus.

This differs from a customer service focus in the sense that all of the previous activities are provided to the customer with the additional support of a customer service process which envelops the customer in pre-sale, during and post-sale activities geared to make the customer experience positive. The customer service process extends into the territory of the customer becoming an advocate for the company.

Customer service, when done well, should appear to the customer to be nearly effortless. I view it as I would the performance of an athlete or a dancer. The moves are graceful and may be extremely difficult. However, the athlete or dancer delivers the routine with well-practiced precision. To me, the parallel is that of the bird of paradise flower.

Behind the graceful delivery of the customer service lies the hard work of process design, planning, practice, execution, culture change, executive champions, reevaluation, training and investment of resources. The work that supports a customer service delivery process is comparable in complexity and effort to the work of the financial or operations sides of the organization.

The objective is clear: Deliver service to your customers with vigor and intent with the objective of making the experience so exceptional that your competition pales in comparison.

So on the delivery side, the customer sees calm, beauty and grace, and experiences the serenity of a bird of paradise. Internally there are intention, focus and high levels of competition, like a bird of prey. – February 21, 2018

6. Communications Capabilities

The ability to communicate is critical to one's existence. We live in an age where the methods of communication have far outpaced one's voice, a letter or, as with many cultures, a musical instrument as primary forms of communication.

It seems that modern society, for the most part, has regulated several communications methods to historical footnotes. I have not heard a horn or drum as an assembly call outside of an outdoor sporting event. The telegram, a communications revolution in its day, has become a niche market — although I find an interesting comparison between telegrams and tweets on Twitter in their speed, brevity and potential for miscommunications. Faxes are also a niche market. Email has all but erased personal letters. Business letters are, in many cases, attachments to an email.

Just one other historical approach that is now marginalized is the use of flags. The U.S. Army's insignia for the Signal Corps is two crossed flags, a form of communication used by armies for centuries.

There are other communications media that have disappeared or are in marginal use. The point today is that communication is not the medium but the message.

We continue to see examples where the message is not clear or consistent and mistakes are made. The leader of your organization and the members of the management team must, where possible, communicate with the team so that the desired actions can be taken. Without the correct messages, resources will be misallocated and management efficiencies can be compromised.

An example I use with clients is to collect the communications from the executive for the past six months. When you read through the communications of all types, you can determine the trends and directions that have been offered. Additionally, you will identify the changes in position and how clearly the rationale for position change was presented to the team. Timing, clarity, rationale and trust are factors tested in each communication.

Managements' perspective, decisions and directions are made in response to market changes. Those messages are translated, by those who receive them, into impact on one's job, area of responsibility, commitments made or other concerns that impact the efficiency of one's work and the organization.

Messaging is not a one-way street. Listening and messaging are connected. For today, we are focusing on messaging, but it's important to call out how vital that connection is.

Executives, members of the management team, in fact all of us should continue to develop our messaging skills for clarity and understanding. We have technologies to communicate more quickly and to more people, but from my observation point, our messaging skill sets have not maintained pace. – June 11, 2017

7. Blind Spots

ecently, my optometrist conducted a field vision test on me. In my case, she was concerned about the potential for me to develop glaucoma. The good news is that the test results were normal.

However, during her review of the examination results, she showed me a graph of my eyes with a small grey area for each eye. She casually identified the grey areas as my "blind spots". She went on to say that everyone has them although the location, shape and size differ from person to person.

Blind spots are real for both cars and people. Numerous automobile manufacturers are delivering technology that will warn the driver when another vehicle is in their blind spot. Most of us have found our blind spots while driving. It is usually the location behind us just over one shoulder or both. It is created because the fields of vision of the rear-view mirror and the side mirrors do not overlap completely. Depending on your vehicle's design elements, the blind spot can be rather small or large enough for an approaching vehicle to become invisible to you for a moment.

So we have visual blind spots and driving blind spots, but what about our other blind spots? Based upon my work with executives across the board, blind spots can be found in other aspects of our lives and particularly in our business lives. For example there are decision-making blind spots. Additionally, there are performance and communications blind spots. There are other categories of blind spots, but let's touch on these three briefly.

Most executives, because of a combination of training, aptitude or preference, make better decisions in one category versus another. Sales or financial decisions may come easily and with accuracy. However, human resources decisions may be a challenge. The difficulty is that the executive may not see his decisions from the perspective of human resources or another department.

A performance blind spot is similar to a decision-making blind spot in the sense that they share functional areas as a base. Additionally, they also are areas where executives tend to have favorites. The difference, however, is that the executive may not be able to see, evaluate or adequately reward because that area has become a bias, and therefore a blind spot. For example, the employee who attended my alma mater, just seems to "get it".

A communications blind spot is very common. We have to communicate as a function of management. However, the elements of communication go beyond word choice. Speech and acting coaches specialize in words and word delivery to improve and promote better communications. Also, our physical presence and appearance start the communications when we enter a room. Think about all the subtle and not so subtle ways we communicate that we have not re-evaluated since high school. This is fertile ground for blind spots.

Once your business coach has helped you to identify your blind spots, there are practices or exercises that might serve to minimize the blind spots. The best solution in many cases may be to hire, retain, marry, befriend or source in some manner a trusted ally who can identify your blind spots and alert you to what is coming in your direction in time for corrective action. – July 11, 2017

8. Automation Competition

utomation is a competitor you do not wish to face in the world of economic competition, while at the same time expecting to win with a human solution.

I was reminded of this during a recent trip to Las Vegas. In one of the countless bars on the famous Las Vegas strip was an automated bartender. The automated bartender had a rack of bottles above the working surface and the technology by robotic standards was relatively straightforward. The drinks, when completed, were delivered to the end of the preparation area by a short conveyor belt, where a human waitresses delivered the drinks to the customers' tables.

News headlines across the country are reporting of the advances being made with driverless cars. The reports often center on the features and benefits of driverless passenger cars. However, the big economic driver and job eliminator potentially will be the driverless trucks that currently deliver all of the goods we consume on a daily basis. I say currently, because some companies are attempting to leapfrog the vehicles and deliver small packages by drones.

It was not that long ago that the first automated teller machines (ATMs) appeared. During those early days of the ATM, very similar concerns were aired about safety of use and security of the transactions. Today most of us use ATMs without a second thought.

Remember when the Internet was scary because we did not want our credit card information moving electronically across the country and around the world. Additionally, I remember hearing concerns about buying clothes and food online because people believed that if they could not touch the items, they could not make the best selections. If the various cyber shopping days are any indication, we have moved past those concerns.

Additionally, brick and mortar stores and salespeople are exposed to significant reductions in numbers. As for food, we not only accept delivery from grocery stores, there is also a growing business of prepared food plans brought to us by meal plan companies.

The concern that I want to bring to your attention is not that automation is bad or that it can be stopped. The issue is what do we do for human jobs when the robotics capabilities continue to improve with lower costs? What happens to people when the computers' artificial intelligence capabilities increase to near-human levels?

To those who say that there will be new positions that will arise for those displaced workers, I say they are partially correct. There is a new team of developers who wrote the applications for the automated bartender. However, they were perhaps a team of ten who by their labor could displace hundreds of bartenders. Also the application development team shrinks to four because it does not take as many people to maintain the application as it did to originally develop the code.

To my knowledge, there is increased automation in nearly every occupational field except among politicians. We need our politicians to address real job issues because we know that retraining, if possible, takes time and money.

Let's have a real debate with real numbers about jobs.

I, for one, like the world of George Jetson but I also remember the story of *John*

Henry, The Steel Driving Man.

The drumbeat of automation continues. Let's be prepared. – August 20, 2017

9. A Business Physical

anaging an organization is not easy or for the faint of heart. Try as we might there are things that are out of our control. In many ways an organization is a living organism similar to each of our lives. So, aside from the acts of nature, accidents, and other complexities of life, there is the increasing amount of information we all have to process.

The processing of information is an area that deserves more attention, but today I will offer an approach to assist in managing some of the information and perhaps reduce some of the risk associated with running an organization.

There are a number of administrative concerns that most organizations have to process on an annual or more regular basis. Insurance is one of those administrative concerns that come to mind. The various insurances that require administrative attention range from health insurance, to perhaps workmen's compensation, to liability and the list goes on.

The utility cost associated with running your organization is an area that bears attention. Additionally, the various software licenses, hardware leases, real estate leases and others usually are on an annual renewal schedule.

Your banking relationship bears an annual review to ensure that your organization's banking needs and the services provided by your bank are aligned. Additionally professional services with your legal counsel, accounting firm, consultants, financial planner and others lend themselves to a formal review on an annual basis.

Taxes, of course, require annual filings and I contend should be followed by an annual plan with your tax preparer for the next year. Tax laws change, and it is best to stay abreast of the impact those changes will have on your organization.

The last area I will mention, but by no means the least or last area of informational concerns for your organization, are your employee policies and plans. Being informed about the laws, policies, personnel trends and how they impact your team, your culture and your success is always important.

Some organizations have staff in each of the above areas whose job is to be current on the subject areas. More organizations outsource some of the functions to professional services companies. Still others rely on industry groups or city and state agencies to provide information and assistance. Some just let it happen and address issues when something is due or worse, when a problem arises.

I have observed that many of these areas of information processing are not coordinated on an annual basis. The recommendation today is for coordinating all of the planning and related activities into one week each year, including: all of the evaluations, license and lease renewals and policy updates and to schedule update lunches with professional services providers. This one week will be the executive physical of your organization.

An executive medical physical can be a multi-day, multi-test, intensive evaluation of your health. It serves to establish a health baseline and can evaluate potential exposures to illnesses not routinely identified in a traditional hour-long physical.

After that one week of intensive review of your organization and a firm plan in place for the next twelve months, some of the stress of managing the organization might be reduced. – May 14, 2017

10. Calendars

Calendars are a key element of most businesses. Many businesses, for example doctors' and dentists' offices, run purely by appointments on calendars dotted with the occasional emergency. In manufacturing, the master production schedule is a calendar that has impact on nearly every decision made in a manufacturing facility. Accountants, attorneys, consultants and other professions, who bill by increments of an hour, use calendars daily.

All organized sporting events and teams work against a calendar. I am sure many of us eagerly anticipate the calendar of our favorite sport to be announced each year. This affords us the opportunity to coordinate our personal calendars so that we may view or attend live events.

We also find calendars in our homes. For many of us, calendars help to manage social engagements, birthdays, medical appointments, vacations and a host of other activities that need to be scheduled and that have priority in our lives. Additionally, if you have children, pets or parents living with you, they may have their own calendars that have to be considered.

Calendars are all around us. How many calendars do you have in your life? Electronic calendars, special calendars, desk calendars, school and favorite charity calendars — when you count them all up, the number may surprise you.

All of us begin with the basic 12-month calendar. We try to anticipate those activities or fixed events that hold priority. Against this neat backdrop comes project deadlines, examinations and audits, new activities and opportunities. Additionally, there is the bad news that also can change a few days on the calendar. However, even with the changes and markups it seems nearly impossible to operate an effective organization without a calendar.

There was a point in time, not that long ago, when there were two means of scheduling time on one's calendar. There was mail and a telephone call. Today, mail seems to be reserved for weddings and graduations. Other than that you can be contacted by any number of communication methods, from telephone to text to social media to calendaring software, with the expectation that once the message is sent, the onus is on the receiver to be at the appointed place on time.

People are different and prefer to be communicated with in different ways. One group I was working with had technical people who declared, "An email is an invitation". Others from the same organization thought that stopping by people's offices to personally invite them to a meeting was a more "relationship based" approach. So, when you distribute your calendar to the organization, consider multiple ways of communicating the information to your team.

The final type of calendar we use is the master calendar. It is important to an organization for many reasons. It will be more comprehensive and when disseminated to the entire organization should increase productivity throughout the year. – June 4, 2016

11. Communications Clarity and Accuracy

Communications is a process that has been studied by many disciplines and we all utilize the studied communications processes every day. Clear, accurate and timely communications are critical to your organization, our country and the world.

In direct terms, this process has three components – input, process and output. The communications process has other components but for brevity, let's stick to the basics. The input is the message that you are sending to me. I, based upon many factors, will process the message. Then, my output can take various forms to include forming an opinion, taking an action or responding with another message. These outputs can be taken individually or in combination.

I have been reminded of the importance of communications by the major events that have occupied the headlines and smaller events in my life over the past few weeks.

The communications surrounding the Ebola epidemic in a few West African nations is the latest example of the importance of communications. Ebola, according to news reports, is not a new disease. Our Federal, State and Local public health officials have monitored the disease for decades. Additionally, the processes and procedures to minimize the impact and spread of the disease are well documented. To this point, I have heard clear, accurate and consistent information from our public health officials.

Weeks ago, there were reports from numerous West African officials and other global health agencies asking for help to contain the spread of the disease. The directive was communicated; however, the required swift action was not.

I recently attended a political forum where candidates for state and federal offices had an opportunity to address an interested audience. During the election season politicians are in sales mode. In this communication convention, the sales mode is a refined form of communications where there is an attempt to present messages in a manner that reflects positively on the politician.

We should be especially attentive when the other speaker is communicating in sales mode.

In another meeting, there were communications regarding the care plan for a loved one. All parties present had specific responsibilities and were working toward the same outcome —the best plan for the benefit of the loved one. There was a clear exchange between all parties of past progress, current assessments and the desired future. Notes were taken and a future meeting was scheduled. This was not the first care plan meeting and the well-established communications process resulted in a successful meeting.

Communications is not easy. Most of us could improve our communications processes. Whether we need better communications regarding the urgency of a health care request or the action items of a care plan for a loved one, I believe improved communications processes will benefit us all. – October 19, 2014

12. Timelines are a Valuable Tool

Timelines are a tool that can be used to represent those activities, accomplishments, events, etc. that occur across a particular span of time. I would imagine, they have been used by individuals, groups and organizations, since the beginning of time.

Timelines represent the story or history of a person, group, culture, subject or organization. How the story is portrayed can vary based upon space, the time period, artistic ability and creativity of the timeline's creators.

In the National Constitution Center, Philadelphia, Pennsylvania, there is a creative and entertaining use of a timeline. The United States Constitution is presented in a timeline. As you walk through the hall you have the opportunity to read the document and reflect on the events and history of our country.

Recently, in a high school classroom, I observed another use of a timeline. It appeared that the students' assignments were hung around the classroom, in sequence of the historic events that represented their assignments. Not only did the students have their work displayed for all to see but they were reminded of the sequence of events every time they were in class. Repetition enhances retention.

Timelines have been introduced to a new generation of users most recently as a feature on one's Facebook page. On that social media site you or your friends can post activities, pictures, etc. on your timeline and thereby create your personal history.

You find timelines occasionally in the lobbies of organizations. Some organizations make use of timelines to decorate their interior spaces and present their history or the development of a particular product. I like this practice because it affords visitors the opportunity to read the history of the organization and thereby have a better understanding of the challenges and successes of the past. It also serves as a motivator for the employees, who can take pride in their part of the organization's story.

At the Subway World headquarters, they have a different slant on a timeline. In their lobby, there are plaques with the names of corporate employees with their start dates, going back to the founder. It is a great reminder that each employee contributed to the organization's past successes.

I have used the concept of a timeline in a group facilitation setting. I had the members of the organization stand in the order in which they joined the organization. The visual was impressive. Then, starting with the most senior members, each team member had a few minutes to tell their story of how the organization functioned when they arrived. The timeline oral history was a powerful tool to get all of the members share their stories and get on the same page.

I have offered a few examples of how you can use timelines to make history a tool. You can inform your teammates and visitors, gain perspectives from the past and promote learning in an approachable manner. – April, 17, 2016

13. Management Treatment of Team Members

Management has final responsibility for what occurs in your organization. On a macro level, culture is one of the key determinants of an organization's success.

Sun Tzu, in his book "The Art of War," states, "Treat your men as you would your own beloved sons. And they will follow you into the deepest valley." To update this ancient text, I'd say, treat your men and your women as your own beloved children.

This quote speaks to the underlying culture of an organization or, in the case of Sun Tzu, a general's army. It is important to point out that treating someone as a beloved son is not to say that one is pampering or not adhering to established policies and procedures.

Firstly, what it does say, to me, is that the management team needs to create a culture where all members of the organization receive, observe and experience the appropriate levels of care, training and guidance. The intention is that all members of the organization are able to achieve their highest potential. With all contributing at their highest potential, the organization will improve its likelihood of success in its chosen endeavor.

You may have experienced the type of leadership Sun Tzu is describing from a coach, or a choir director, or in the military. Most strong organizations have multiple levels of managers who, in their own ways, subscribe to this principle of Sun Tzu. From my observations, the size of the organization and the industry does not matter. If this principle is consciously implemented by the leadership, it will be followed.

Think about your own leaders or those you have followed in the past. The specific techniques and approaches may have differed from one leader to another. However, upon review, you may find that your feelings motivated you to stay the course and contribute at a high level.

Secondly, a clear understanding of the rules and guidelines of the organization go a long way toward establishing a culture where one can feel beloved. Going hand in hand with understanding is the consistent administration of consequences across the organization when one does not adhere to those rules and guidelines. Not many people appreciate favoritism or the acceptance of slacking. The discipline to correct a team member in a timely and suitable manner is a well-known art and science to parents and to effective leaders.

The development of a person is important to the individual and to the organization. The time investment, goal-setting, training and encouragement are just a few of the characteristics necessary to move a person's skills and capabilities to a higher level. Once again, it is creating the environment or culture that allows each member of the organization to grow into that person's skills and capabilities.

Lastly, the management team should regularly review how the organization's culture is creating the environment where all members feel beloved and are willing to follow, being fully engaged. – March 6, 2016

14. Employee Playbook

T here are many parallels that can be drawn between American football, as played by the National Football League, and the world of business.

For the past several years, there has been a reality television show following one team during the training camp period leading up to the start of the season. I have watched the program for years and have noticed a change in a fundamental area critical to the success of the team — the playbook.

In early shows the playbook was a large three-ring binder. The playbook, as the name indicates, includes the formations and plays that the team will utilize during the course of the season. In addition to plays, there is information unique to each team, for example: nomenclature, organization charts and other information necessary for each player to be a contributing member of the team. In recent years, players had a laptop computer or tablet that contained the playbook information.

In business, one element of your playbook or policy manual is the employees' handbook. An organization's policy manual is the overarching document that defines operational boundaries across multiple functions. The employees' handbook is a subset of the policy manual. Some of you may have just rolled your eyes at the thought of updating your employees' handbook or in the worst case creating one.

Just as in football, you need to have all of your team on the same page. Your team needs to have an accurate and current understanding of the boundaries and the consequences for stepping across them.

Creating or updating an employee handbook is labor intensive but worth the effort. If you do not have a cadre of Human Resource (HR) professionals on your team, I suggest contacting your accountant, attorney, Chamber of Commerce or a local HR Consultant to ask for assistance. Also, as with most things, you can do a search on the internet to gain some ideas on the subjects to include in your employees' handbook.

A point to be taken from the football teams. The handbooks, which actually were a pamphlet in some organizations, lend themselves well to electronic delivery. An internal document, with an opening by the team leader on your website for internal use only, might be the right play to get your team working together.

Books have been written on employees' handbooks. Two final points: First, the employees' handbook documents how your organization will operate. The documentation is the written foundation of your organization's culture. Second, when there is a challenge to your organization, whether from legal channels, a regulatory body's inquires or a team member's concern, the employee handbook is one of your key lines of defense.

 - September 7, 2014

15. Personal and Business Challenges

The year-end festivities and crunch are behind us. From a business perspective, for those using an annual fiscal year, the performance of 2014 is history.

For many organizations the operational planning process is in full swing. There are planning sessions where performance objectives are being set, personnel objectives are being communicated to the team and the financial plan is being adjusted for maximum achievement. Most of us are optimistic about the future, and we are also planning for those potential negatives.

On the personal level, some people develop resolutions to change their lives in the New Year. One of the leading resolutions is that of losing weight and/or getting in better physical shape. If the marketing campaigns are any indication, this is the high season for new gym memberships. I know a few people who are gym regulars who take the first two weeks off in January to allow the resolution members to come and burn out. My friends return by the end of the month when the gym is not as crowded with people who have abandoned their resolutions.

I have observed that this year a number of the daytime television personalities offering various challenges to their viewers. Weight loss, dietary improvements and relationship development seem to be among the top three.

Beyond television, there appears to be an increase in challenges. Recall last summer the ice bucket challenges. As a motivational tool, friends on social media are challenging each other with daily updates for planking, distance walking, push-ups, and the list goes on.

Many in business might say, "Our business objectives are a challenge. That should be enough for the team to be inspired." We can all make that claim. However, what business would not benefit from a fast start with new clients, new infrastructure or new skills coming on line?

An internal challenge can be a way to motivate your team beyond the line items in their performance plans. Key elements of a well-designed challenge are that it has to be achievable, connected to your success factors, limited in duration and with well communicated rules and objectives. It should also provide the opportunity for the entire team and have an incentive consistent with your values and resources.

The challenge could be designed for the entire organization or for a manager's department. The challenge design might benefit from the team's input after the yearly or quarterly objectives are clearly identified. Additionally, the challenge should be easy to keep score and should be fun.

Also, if you have held challenges before, learn from what worked well with your team and what did not. A review of the Internet for challenges will yield a host of ideas to serve as starters that can be modified to suit your organization's needs.

A well designed challenge could build morale, increase business and increase your organization's momentum based upon the quick start generated. – January 11, 2015

16. We are all Customers

We are all customers and at the same time we are all providing services to others in our business or personal lives. Our breadth of services may range from the highest professional levels of saving a life or expanding a student's understanding to the most simple but significant action of listening to a friend.

Playing both roles, the question I ask is—"What matters in providing quality customer service?" My formal and informal research over the last five years has yielded five elements of the answer. The elements of—timely service, knowledge, communications, respect and trust are repeated most often across a broad range of professional and personal customer service environments.

Time is the friend and enemy of us all. It plays a major role when it comes to providing quality customer service. Think of the wonderful buying experience you might have at a local warehouse club. They probably have fed you, you have purchase hibernation sizes of items you need and now you are ready to check out and....wait. We want our customer service to be efficient with our time throughout the entire customer service experience. Waiting in long lines is not in any of our definition of quality customer service.

Time, however, works at both ends of the customer service interaction. Based on our time schedule, we may want to discuss the latest digital photography features at our leisure, but when we have made our decision, the purchase transaction needs to be very fast. Basically, we want the timeliness of our customer service to be fast or slow depending upon our schedules and interests.

Knowledge of the service or product being offered speaks for itself. I have found that when a service provider does not have the correct answer it is desirable and even admirable to admit that you do not have the final answer. But the next step is critical, we then want the customer service provider to research the answer and get back with us in a timely fashion. I was recently in a Staples retail store in Stratford, and the person I spoke with could not answer my question. However, he took me to a computer, looked up the product specifications and was then able to answer the question. He made the sale based upon the quality customer service he delivered to me that day.

Communications is frequently a critical element in what matters in customer service. How often have you had a quality customer service experience and no one communicated with you afterwards? Not often. Communications is necessary to begin a quality relationship and that relationship is the foundation of the other customer service elements.

Respect is easy to know when you have it and easier to know when you don't. Courtesy and respect go hand in hand. Most of the time when you visit the South we are confronted with something we don't hear often in Connecticut. Almost everywhere you go, you can hear, "Yes, 'Mam or No, Sir." Customer service wrapped in respect and courtesy makes it complete.

The final element—trust is the hardest to obtain, the easiest to loose and the most important to keeping a customer today and tomorrow. Trust continues to be high in survey results because we all want it in all aspects of our lives. How often do you give your business to someone you do not trust? Each customer service opportunity adds or subtracts from the trust you have built with that customer.

The combination of the above customer service elements depends on the industry, culture, geography and training. Whether we are providing or receiving service our goal should be to offer the highest level of each element and the result will be what matters in quality customer service. − June 25 1010

17. Value of Surveys

C ustomer service should be a cornerstone of every organization. A quality product or service, financial controls and a qualified staff are the other elements of a successful organization.

In some organizations, customer service is not viewed as critical to the organization's mission. For those organizations that choose to compete on the basis of their customer service, the voice of the customer impacts all of their service-related decisions.

Regardless of the driving force of the organization—product or service, low cost, or customer focus, it is critical for the organization to maintain an awareness of its environment. One popular technique is the use of surveys.

Most of us have participated in the development and distribution of a survey at some point. Asking a group of friends what type of pizza to order is a functional and quick survey technique. At the other end of the spectrum are sophisticated surveys designed by academics or marketing specialists.

The varieties of surveys have continued to evolve over time. Perhaps the most famous surveys are those conducted by the federal government every 10 years—the United States Census. This traditional model of survey taker, client and paper surveys is still efficient and effective.

The techniques associated with the contact and distributions of surveys have evolved, in large part due to technology. Most of us have seen the comment card surveys at a local restaurant or hotel. Recently, I participated in a survey from a cell phone company that called my cell phone. A friendly, automated voice asked me to complete a five-question survey. Technology had moved surveys into another distribution model.

Surveys can also be found on your receipt from purchases. Additionally, some receipts have web sites or telephone numbers, usually with an incentive, if you access a website and take a survey. Nearly every online purchase will yield a survey sent to your email. Some organizations offer a brief survey at the end of a telephone transaction. I have found this to be especially true when you are calling about a customer service issue.

Your organization may already use surveys to gain customer insight, or you may be considering a new survey initiative. Let me offer a few suggestions that might improve your participation and engagement with your customers. First, develop a process for handling the information from the surveys in a manner that can result in changes to your organization. Second, notify your customers when a new process or actions were the result of survey input. Finally, combine a personal touch via a telephone call, or email chat with a sampling of your customers.

Customer needs and wants are critical to the success of a customer service strategy. Surveys should be a technique of your customer assessment process. – March 10, 2013

18. Business Science

Today is October 10, 2010, according to one date-writing format. For my binary readers this is pretty cool. The reason I bring this to your attention is that there have been a number of symbolic attachments to this day.

Many people around the world have set this day aside as a Day of Doing. The Day of Doing is a day of individual actions that will have a positive impact on the environment. According to the Day of Doing website, the act of doing something by people, without government support, may spur policy makers to be more proactive about addressing climate issues.

There are traditional sciences like physics, biology, and chemistry, etc. and there is business science like the bottom line of your organization. Regardless of your scientific perspective on global warming, let's take a look at the business science or the bottom line of global warming you should consider.

I have been associated with the information technology industry for a few decades. The promise and delivery of the "paperless office" has been with us for many years. However, most organizations are still up to their filing cabinets in paper. So for your Day of Doing, later this week, ask your team to start duplex printing (printing on both sides) all documents. Internal documents should be easy. Additionally, for those meeting agendas, jokes, interesting websites, etc., those documents will print comfortably on the back of a previously printed, non-confidential piece of paper. You may not be able to reduce your paper usage by half but there will be reductions in paper usage. There are three major benefits to these actions: 1) your paper costs will be reduced; 2) fewer trees will be cut to produce paper and; 3) less water will be used to produce paper. Trees produce oxygen and water is becoming globally scarce.

A number of organizations have initiated private bus transportation from major transportation hubs, such as the train station, to their work locations. If you cannot afford a private bus, evaluate the public transportation option for those employees who can get to your location on public transportation. There may be a number of programs that might support this activity. The benefits of this activity include less energy usage, employees who do not come to work with "road rage" and perhaps assistance to make it happen.

Electricity usage has been on the forefront of environmental concerns from the beginning. Electricity is one of the pillars of our society. Being efficient with our usage is good business science. If you have a roof, install solar panels. These type of panels have been proven to reduce energy consumption from the electrical grid. President Obama is installing solar panels on the White House. I think that is a pretty clear message to our nation and to the world.

If you cannot afford solar panels or do not have a roof, ask your local utility company to conduct an energy audit of your business. The audits are for the most part free and in many cases the cost of implementation of the recommendations will be solid business science and rapidly recovered in energy savings.

Now that you have done something to preserve the environment and save yourself some money, take the next step—tell your customers. If you have reduced the carbon footprint of your organization, let your customers know. If you have reduced your costs, give a bonus to those team members who initiated the idea or are sustaining the work. If you get a tax credit or deductions for an energy program, notify your elected representatives that one program is working. Customers make decisions to buy for many reasons. Provide them with one more reason to buy from you. Tell them your organization is doing something positive for their environment. Then you can breathe a little easier with business science on your side. - October 10, 2010

19. Executive Coach

For sport fans, this is a great time of year. Baseball is in full swing. Basketball and hockey are finally in their playoff seasons. The Women's National Basketball Association (WNBA) has begun its season. Formula 1 and The National Association for Stock Car Auto Racing (NASCAR) are thrilling their crowds. Golf and tennis pros are prowling the warmer venues. Track and field festivals, among others, are preparing our athletes for the Olympics.

What all of these varied sports have in common are coaches. Coaches are most evident in sporting venues but, they are becoming increasingly visible and appreciated in the halls of business. Business coaching and life coaching are no longer fads. They are now seen as an important requirement if you want to reach the top of your game.

The reason for business coaches is the same reason that athletes need coaches—to improve individual and team performance. The areas of business performance are many and dependent on both. Management, the art and science that often determines business success, is an area where business coaches have worked with clients for decades.

We all have a set of skills that have allowed us to move up the ranks or grow our businesses. In most cases, those skills are technical skills we gained through formal education, or we may be blessed with a particular talent. However, sometimes before we can make that next move there is some aspect of our "game" that is preventing our advancement. Some of the areas that business coaches focus on with business athletes could be people skills, salesmanship, strategic thinking, delegation, time management or other areas of refinement. Business coaching can play a big role in "rounding out" an executive.

Actually, sports coaching is in some ways easier than business coaching. One of the reasons we are drawn to sports is that regardless of your favorite sporting contest, the entire event is presented to you in about a three hour drama. Techniques, strategies, emotions, equipment, attack and counterattack, and finally, hopefully good sportsmanship are portrayed before your very eyes. In the sports world, the coach can make recommendations in real time, evaluate the success or failure, and at the conclusion of the contest, know what to work on at practice the next day.

Business is not a neat, rule-based, timed event. It is continuous and fluid. So, the business coach has to work with the business athlete on those areas that need improvement and accept the feedback in the blind, because when the event occurs the coach is usually not present.

For example, an executive may have an important presentation to make to a key client. A business coach is hired to improve the executive's presentation skills. The business coach follows the same approach as the sports coach. Typically he would evaluate the business athlete's current capabilities, develop goals for improvement, create a proactive regimen of skill development and provide motivation. However, after all of the sweat and work, the business coach is usually not at the presentation. The business coach has to rely on the report from the business athlete. Real-time observation is a major advantage.

As with sports, the primary reasons for business coaching are that the stakes are higher and the competition is intense from across the street and around the world. To be successful a business athlete has to master many business skills similar to that of a decathlete's mastery of 10 track and field events. Tiger Woods, one of the world's best golfers, has a coach. Are you better in your game than Tiger is in his? A coach can help you reach your potential and improve your business. – October 25, 2010

43

20. Everyone Sells

When I attended a sales conference a few years ago, one of the presenters proclaimed, "Everybody sells".

His statement has come back to my mind frequently. In every marketing or sales course I have taught, sometime during the semester I recall that marketing battle cry. I can only hope my students have held onto the statement as I have.

Businesses today—and in fact our entire society—are in constant sales mode. All media, all the time, by all sources are marketing, spinning or selling us something. Even when we are told there is no spin, there is spin. Truly, we are in a hyper-selling environment.

Organizations and industries not typically associated with selling are now directly and indirectly utilizing marketing techniques that are promoting their products and services. Hospitals have large billboards and radio spots touting their special rankings on some list that sounds very important. Higher education institutions are in constant sell mode and at the price of education, each student represents a nice contract.

My oil change location recently sent me a postcard stating that by texting them, I would be entered into a contest. I rarely win anything, but my lack of success does not prevent me from participating in most contest offers I encounter. In the near future, they will be selling me via text directly to my cell phone.

In your organization, you have the opportunity to mobilize your silent sales force—your non-sales employees. I am speaking of casual sales, not the sales capabilities that result from years of professional development. However, with a few simple steps, you can start to engage all of your employees to make a sales difference in these challenging times.

The first item to be addressed is that your employees have to be proud of your organization. If they feel they are treated fairly, your products or service are high quality and that you usually provide quality customer service, they will be more inclined to support the organization. Even in casual sales, we put our personal reputation on the line. So being positive and proud of your organization is critical.

In years past, it seems that more people wore the caps or jackets of their place of business. Instead of our organization's polo shirt, we wear sport shirts of favorite teams or designers. So, the second action to take is to provide tasteful and attractive items that allow your employees to be walking billboards for your organization.

Everyone needs a business card to exchange. I will talk more about business cards in a future column. Suffice to say that the cost of the cards will surely result in additional recognition and, hopefully, business.

Only the best of salespeople, can "sell out of an empty cart". So, you must prepare your employees with information about your organization. From a new menu item to a green product line extension that will save customers' time and money, your employees should be aware of your business trends. If your employees are familiar with the business, then they can be comfortable talking about it.

We are well into the summer season of cookouts, sporting activities and vacations. I am not suggesting that all employees will become non-stop sales people. That mission belongs to the sales staff and the executive team. However, I am suggesting that when the casual conversation turns to—"So, where do you work?" or "How are things going at your place?"—they are prepared and want to say something positive. If you have not prepared them with a response that will benefit your organization and them directly or indirectly, then you have missed a sales opportunity. Because..."Everyone can sell." - July 3, 2009

21. Strengths, Weaknesses, Opportunities and Threats (SWOT) Analysis for the New Year

The New Year often brings new perspectives and hopes of new personal and business successes. As individuals, many of us make New Year's resolutions. But for a business, often the best resolution is to develop or modify the organization's strategic plan.

The strategic plan is the document in the back of the filing cabinet, which supposedly guides our actions for the year and probably hasn't been touched since last year. It may be time for a checkup or a SWOT analysis.

A SWOT analysis is a snapshot in time of your business, operation or an individual. SWOT stands for Strengths, Weaknesses, Opportunities and Threats. This planning technique has been around since the 1960's and is credited to Albert Humphrey and his research at Stanford University.

Typically, the strengths and weaknesses are those factors that are internal to the organization, and opportunities and threats evaluate external factors. When viewed in combination, the four SWOT dimensions present a picture of the organization and its business environment. Many planning techniques have come and gone, but the SWOT analysis continues to deliver a lot of value for minimal investment.

All businesses develop plans. The question is the depth of the planning, time frame of the process and other resources involved in the process. General Electric, for example, has a planning process that is continuously modified and updated. Its plans are multi-level, detailed and include all of its business units around the world. Most organizations do not have the resources to make that level of commitment to planning.

A SWOT analysis is on the other end of the planning spectrum. It can be used as a beginning of the strategic planning process. A SWOT analysis can be used as an annual update to a formal strategic planning process to determine whether the organization is on target. For a large number of organizations the plan offered from a SWOT analysis, developed over a relatively short period of time, will serve as a solid foundation for the year.

An annual SWOT analysis is similar to an annual physical or checkup. We spend an hour or two at the doctor's office, our vital signs are reviewed, certain standard tests are performed, our blood gets analyzed and few days later we hopefully get a satisfactory report. Nearly always there are words of caution from the doctor regardless of how well we have been since our last physical. Our business lives will benefit from an annual checkup as well.

A friend of mine mentioned that he had developed a number of personal plans or resolutions for 2008. When asked how he was doing with them, he first took a drink, smiled and stated, "I just broke another one." The interesting thing about resolutions and plans is that they have to be realistic. If my friend had looked internally, he would have recognized he has both strength and a weakness for being in a social environment where he enjoys beverages. Additionally, he would have recognized that some business conversations and opportunities are held in such social environments. And third, there might be a threat to his social and business standing in the community if he is not visible. A SWOT analysis might have shown my friend that his energy to maintain that resolution might be better placed elsewhere. The same kind of analysis can benefit your business.

A New Year's resolution is not the best way to run your business. However, a SWOT analysis can turn those resolutions into realistic plans that can sustain you for the year and beyond. - January 20, 2008

22. Customer Service can be Free

Most business people are talking about how difficult it is to do business in today's environment. The business press and related media outlets are presenting stories on the credit squeeze, declines in consumer confidence and rising levels of unemployment. The list of concerns continues.

For most companies doing more with fewer employees has become the new culture. Most find it difficult to raise prices and there is intense competition from next door and around the world. With many business indicators trending in a negative direction, it is difficult to see an opportunity. In the face of these factors, let me suggest that now is the perfect time to reevaluate and improve your customer service. In fact, improving your customer service may be one of the last management tools left in the tool box to improve your business' performance.

Customer service fits between all the effort, time and money you expend to acquire a new customer and the need to continue and expand the business relationships you have with your existing customers. On one side, customer service is critical to the growth of the business and on the other side we do not pay it the attention it deserves. To prove the point how much effort do you expend to positively maintain your friendships?

To renew your focus on customer service, let me suggest a few first steps. Customer service starts with people and in most situations, it will end with people. Recognize that your team needs to refocus its understanding on the value of improving the customer service it provides. The best way to start that improvement is with a pep talk.

In February, all Starbucks Coffee shops across the country closed for two hours to be trained on new products and to get a pep talk on the value of customer service from the CEO. Two hours! At the end of that time, do you feel there were any questions in the employees' minds of how important customer service is to their business? Also, if you can't effectively deliver the pep talk, hire someone who can deliver it for you.

Taking two hours from production to focus on customer service is amazing, yet the same thing can be accomplished around the lunch room table. There are other methods to get the message out to the team. Recently in the NCAA basketball championships, we saw the benefits of taking a time out and having the team huddle. The key to success of the huddle is that the top of the business must be committed, the message must be clear as to the importance of customer service, and the message must be enthusiastic. Enthusiasm is contagious and works.

Additionally, focus on the simple things that we learned a long time ago, yet perhaps don't practice as much as we should. Smile and say "please" and "thank you". Most customers still appreciate these timeless foundations of customer service.

The final point is to take a quick review of your customer service procedures to ensure they are consistent with the way you wish to run your business. As you review the procedures, put yourself in the customer's position and ask yourself, "Is this how I would want to be treated as a customer?" Make changes as necessary.

Consider that a smile, a pep talk, a huddle and a re-evaluation of how you treat customers can improve your customer service. Customer service can directly improve customer retention, which improves profitability. The best news, in this tight business environment, is that the above items and the associated customer service improvements can be free. – September 25, 2010

23. Praise in Public

I had a conversation about management techniques with a friend who was a former employee and manager at International Business Machines (IBM).

Our conversation led to one of the first lessons taught in "New Managers' School". That lesson was: Praise in public and criticize in private. I had experienced that management philosophy at the company before I attended "New Managers' School". After being taught that approach, I and all the IBM managers I observed followed that credo.

Back in those days at IBM, every new manager within their first month as a first-line manager, had to attend New Manager's School. The school was a full week and it was held in a divisional or corporate headquarters location. To my recollection, it was the same training for all divisions in the company. That was quite an investment in the new manager and by extension the personnel reporting to that manager. This focus on manager development, among other things, helped IBM to be considered by some in the business press to be one of the best managed corporations in the world.

Praise in public is direct and to the point. Most of us, if recognized in front of our peers like to be praised for a positive accomplishment. The benefit to the individual is clear and is usually followed by further congratulations by their peers. A second benefit to this approach is that it's clear to the team the level of accomplishment that is worthy of public praise. This action is setting the standard and thereby influencing the culture of achievement in your organization. The third benefit of this approach, is that management will receive credit from the team for recognizing the hard work and sacrifice that usually precedes most significant accomplishments.

To criticize in private follows a similar path of personnel management. Being criticized by a manager in front of one's peers rarely leaves a good feeling with the employee. Secondly, the level that warrants management criticism will erode the confidence of others. They will tend to avoid approaching that level that resulted in their fellow employee being publicly chastised. Fear of making a mistake is the exact opposite condition of what is necessary to create an innovative corporate culture.

Finally, try as we may as managers we do not know all of the details and backstories of a given situation. A private conversation can bring to light items that might influence your assessment of the team member's performance. If you had criticized a team member publicly, such reprimands, when known by other team members, could undermine your leadership role and erode your team's trust in you. I terminated my relationship with a dentist because he chastised a team member in front of the team and patients.

I present this basic management lesson in all of my classes, seminars or coaching relationships. It is not easy to adhere to this approach yet the effort is worth the result.

– June 28, 2015

24. Communications Needs

Management is responsible for the communications culture in the organization. The Communications culture encompasses clarity, completeness, speed and appropriateness of the communications in an organization. There are many elements of organizational culture. Communications is the most basic – it is even a predictor of success.

The clarity of communications depends a great deal on the organization type. The military, legal and healthcare industries come to mind quickly as organizations in which communications among colleagues must be clear. Listening to doctors talk about the status of a patient is a model of clarity and brevity of communications. Each of the respective industries have members who work and have been trained in the language particular to their industry. Additionally, they recognize that time is a critical factor in communications among colleagues. Communications in these industries is akin to a relay team's smooth exchange to ensure a team's success.

Another element of clarity can happen when you communicate your true assessment of a situation. Effective management establishes the need and freedom for communications to be clear. The need comes from the notion that acting upon unclear or incomplete communications can result in a wrong decision being made resulting in misallocated company resources.

Freedom of communication is based upon the old expression ,"Don't shoot the messenger." A few moments of reflection will allow a manager to recall whether he or she is guilty of this communications dam. If you do not allow your team members to communicate their honest feelings you may miss important understanding about given situations. More importantly, you may inadvertently shut down a member of your team from giving their best. After all, sometimes we deliver bad news, and each team member will sometimes even disagree with management's direction.

Completeness in communications involves providing as much information as necessary for the listener to understand the message. The vital facts may be another way to present the completeness of communications. A manager can practice this with the team. When a given situation is presented, one that will be repeated, have one member of the team give a report in front of the team. With additional questioning, the team can gain insight into the specific types of information that will result in complete communications.

Speed is a question of timeliness. Most of us can think of a story when the lack of timely communications caused a problem. However, there is a balance that needs to be struck between speed and completeness. I found that a reasonable compromise is for the communications to be dated and the omitted or incomplete information noted.

Appropriateness of communications is a much bigger issue than this space allows. However, one element is the quantity of e-mail communications that do not contribute to information moving forward. You know the kind — reply all, mass distribution lists and confirmations of receipt to name a few.

A culture of better communications will improve the work environment and ultimately organizational outcomes.

25. Checklists

There are a number of ways to provide clients with a feeling of support and engagement. One simple approach you might consider to ensure a consistent client experience is to create a checklist.

Checklists have been around for a long time and their uses range from the weekly shopping list to the pre-flight checklist that pilots routinely go through before every flight. Checklists have also been found in operating rooms, board rooms and classrooms. The applications for checklists are seemingly endless.

We use checklists in our daily lives. Most of the time, we do not formalize or write the checklists down because they are highlighting daily routines. Your morning regimen is an activity that lends itself to a checklist. However, most of us do not have our morning checklist posted on the bathroom mirror.

You can consider using a checklist for a new activity that you wish to have consistency and a specific desired outcome. The next time you have a new project consider introducing a checklist.

On a recent business trip, I encountered a number of checklists. Checklists were visible in the cockpits of the airplanes on my trip. I created a checklist for the trip because of the number of flights, car rentals, security system panels and hotel rooms on the trip. It was a great way to keep me on schedule and moving in the right direction.

I noticed that in the hotels as I was checking in, each of the front desk personnel went through a well-rehearsed checklist of information pertaining to my stay at their property. In prior hotel stays, you might recall that the bellman, while waiting for you to get your baggage tip ready, walked you through a number of items to showcase the room. Heating controls, shower controls and television remote and stations were usually on the room orientation checklist.

As we enter into the Holiday Season, you may find yourself with guests in your home. I have noticed that each house has a different orientation and amenities. There was a time when visiting a friend or family was very basic. Light switches were up and down and water faucets were hot and cold. Not so any more. Think about the checklist that might be helpful for your guests. Light switches, television controls, music controls, heating controls, microwave and cooking top controls are just a few of the things in your home that might be items on a guests' checklist.

As you work through your holiday decorating or shopping checklists, think about how the simple yet functional technique might be useful in your organization. Checklists might help your associates be more comfortable in the execution of a new activity and your clients to experience more consistent outcomes.

Making a list and checking it twice...Happy holidays!- December 13, 2012

26. Robots and Jobs

Two weeks ago on the CBS television program *60 Minutes*, one program segment discussed the growth in robots in our society. The story was positioned to view the robots as competition for jobs.

Robots, as presented in the program, included physical robots that have become all too common in manufacturing facilities, software as presented in automated answering systems with voice recognition capabilities and even robots that have found their way into operating theaters to assist in delicate surgeries. Also, computer stock trading software was presented as robots replacing jobs.

If you are a regular reader of this column, you know my distaste for "robotic" check-out lines. Additionally, I have mentioned the loss of toll operator positions to the radio frequency interface devices many of us have in our cars. You can add to the list of robotic job displacers, ATM terminals and ticket kiosks at movie theaters and airline counters.

Even your smart phone could be viewed as a replacement for a job. Not long ago there were devices called personal digital assistants which had only a few of the apps that we now associate with a smart phone. Your smartphone's daily tasks used to be a job for a person.

On a recent road trip through Ohio, I passed a Ford Motor company plant located along the interstate. I have driven past this plant for decades. In the past, the sprawling factory's parking lot was full of employees' automobiles, mostly Ford cars. On this trip, however, barely 30 percent of the parking spaces were occupied.

You can add to the robot list the IBM Watson Computer that beat human champions at the television game show *Jeopardy*. It has been reported that a software program can now write a simple baseball sports story with only the game's statistics as input. Perhaps the ultimate human replacements are robotic avatar blackjack dealers in casinos.

So, based upon the above tally of robots versus humans, we have factory workers, receptionists, surgeons, sports writers, stock traders, bank tellers, store cashiers, *Jeopardy* contestants, casino blackjack dealers, movie ticket personnel, toll collectors and airline counter staff as human positions being displaced. Every day new jobs are being added to the list.

I understand the need for managers to be effective and efficient. Briefly stated, effective means to remain competitive and profitable, and efficient is to do so with the minimal amount of resources or cost. Taking those management core beliefs just a few decades or even years from now and I can envision a society with the need for very few human jobs. A great deal of work will be done but it will be more efficient and effective to do it with a variety of robots.

There is an American folktale of John Henry the steel driving man. We cannot reverse being efficient and effective. The robots will win. Perhaps we need to re-define human work. What do you think? - September 22, 2013

27. Sharpen Your Tools

If you are among those who for reasons of practicality, love of nature or expense management, do your own spring yard cleanup, it is time to sharpen your tools. I am referring to those tools that we use to improve our outdoor and our business surroundings. We must keep our business tools sharp.

After an early spring grass cut with a dull lawnmower blade, I have been clubbing my grass instead of cutting it. It was time to sharpen my lawnmower blade. So, in preparation for my outdoor spring rituals, I took my lawnmower blade to my favorite tool-sharpening business.

I like this business because it is one of the best in New England and provides great customer service. I usually go to the company in the spring and fall. Nearly every time I visit the company, I arrange a tour of the facility. Without fail, the tour presents something new and different. It is clear that they continue to sharpen their business tools.

The company seems to be constantly in motion. The work centers are continually evaluated and relocated to improve work flow. In some areas of the business, miraculous machines from foreign manufactures move to computer commands and expand the service offerings of the company. Additional services usually yield additional revenues and improved customer engagement.

Although the business is changing in many ways, it is still grimy and hard physical work. However, this company is mixing old and new technologies with semiskilled labor and highly skilled labor in an amazing manner.

As with my favorite tool sharpening company, each of our business environments needs to plant seeds of change to grow and develop new skills. Business tools and skills sharpening could be a refreshed website, additional online service offerings or catalogues, and revised relationships with suppliers. Sometimes an examination of your sales and marketing processes can sharpen that critical area of your business. Assessing the business tools and skills you need to hone should be a part of your annual business plan. In my relationship with this cutting company, I see tangible change and improvement in cycles of six to nine months. Can your customers say the same thing about your business?

Sharpened business skills and their benefits are not limited to organizations. Each individual in the organization should have the opportunity for skill development and growth. Skill development can be an investment that yields nearly immediate benefits to the individual and the organization.

There is the story, from the northwestern United States, of the man with a slightly muscular physique who applies for a job as a lumberjack. At this time before chainsaws, the foreman questions the man's ability to do the job considering the pro-football dimensions of the current crew of lumberjacks. To get the job, the foreman challenges the man to a day-long contest to chop as much wood as one of the larger men in the crew. At the end of the day, the lumberjack's pile of wood measured 13-feet high and the applicant's pile was 13-feet, 6-inches high. The foreman offered the job to the man with the only condition being that he tells how he was able cut so much wood. The man's reply was, "Sometimes, you have to stop and sharpen your tools."

Every one of us has sharpened our skills either formally or informally throughout our business careers. At this time, I am suggesting that we take a new look at our needs and make a conscious effort to sharpen our skills. You need to have sharp tools to cut grass or succeed in business. - October 25, 2010

28. Managers as Role Models

Management is an old art and a relatively new science. Among the cornerstones of management is the requirement of the manager to serve as a role model.

We hear constantly in the media about whether a particular person is a good or a bad role model. In my opinion applying the title of role model to various actors, athletes, business people or even politicians is a stretch. It is a stretch because we cannot and do not know the pressures or situations that got them to make the decisions they made, both good and bad. No one is perfect.

However, managers are expected to be role models for the organization. We do have additional insight on some but not all of the circumstances that impact their behavior. I believe management's responsibility as role model is most critical in the guidance and direction of new and young employees. In your past, you might find managers, who by their actions, influenced you and your management style.

We have all had good managers and those who needed improvement. We hope the managers we experienced were honest and dealt with their colleagues with integrity. If a manager does not meet that minimum requirement, then he or she should be removed from their position. Removal will be best for the organization. Not only is that behavior not good for internal relations, but also it can damage relationships with your customers and suppliers.

Let's assume that the other key elements of a good manager are in place—intelligence, organizational awareness, decision making skills, etc., so we can focus on the aspects of a role model. We observe the way managers interact with people, how they dress, how they show empathy or not. As a manager you are on public display. This constant observation by your staff is a burden, an opportunity and why managers get paid the big bucks. Really.

During difficult times it is hard to be a good role model. I am familiar with an organization experiencing potential layoffs. One manager called in to volunteer to be moved to another department. On the surface it appears to be a personal sacrifice, but upon closer inspection it was abandoning the ship. The situation was contained and the manager's request was not made public to his staff.

During our recent winter, managers across our area had numerous opportunities to be role models. How did you balance the responsibility of work with the hazards imposed by the snow? A friend of mine, after shoveling snow for two hours, had his son drive him to work. The son worked for the father and drove an SUV that could make it safely to the office. The son had thought it would be a snow day. The father as manager had to be a role model for a more responsible outcome.

We do not expect our managers to be perfect role models. However, we appreciate a reasonable amount of predictability—just as a pitcher, batter and catcher in baseball expect predictability in the umpire's calls of balls and strikes. There are general guidelines but room for personal interpretation. Consistency leads to predictability, one pitch to another and one management situation to another.

My counsel for managers is to first remember that you are being observed all the time. Since you are being observed, get the basics right consistently. Attire, time management, timing of decision-making and analysis all help to provide the predictability that is an important part in being a role model. As mentioned above, also maintain a positive attitude and try to consider others' well-being in all your decisions.

What is on your management's role model checklist? - May 22, 2011

29. Teamwork Example

We all know the story of *Rudolph the Red-Nosed Reindeer.* The story goes that Santa Claus has a team of reindeer ready to deliver Christmas presents. However, due to inclement weather he was concerned that he would not be able to complete his mission. Then Rudolph, with a unique but unappreciated talent, became a critical member of the team and guided Santa Claus and the rest of the team to a successful night of worldwide deliveries.

There are many stories of people working together to accomplish significant tasks. Teams and teamwork have and will continue to be, for the foreseeable future, the best way to accomplish more than the sum of the parts. Here is one recent story of teamwork that is suitable for this holiday season.

I am familiar with an organization that has a policy that provides all employees with vacation and sick days. One of the employees was recently diagnosed with cancer. One of the life complications of the illness is a six-week period of treatments where the person would not be able to work. Most organizations cannot and do not allow employees enough sick days for such an extended time. The combination of illness, treatments and the unfortunate loss of income is a stressful mixture. Just imagine.

The members of her team got together to discuss what could be done to support the stricken team member. One member of the team suggested that each member of the organization donate one of their sick days and create a pool of sick days to cover the time the ill employee would be away. Management was made aware of the team's desires and not only supported the activity, but also participated with each member of the management team personally donating a day to the pool.

When the ill person formally announced to her team that she would have to leave for six weeks of treatment, she was surprised by a gift from her fellow team members of a package of donated sick days. The total sick days were equal to the six weeks that the stricken employee would be away from work for treatments. The result was that there would be no loss of income for the family. I was not there, but I can believe that there was not a dry eye in the room.

The story continues. The ill team member has a child in the day care at the organization. The grandmother drops off and picks up the child every day. The other team members have set up a schedule where each of them prepares a little more food than usual and then presents the grandmother with a dish every day when she picks up her grandchild. This has been going on for weeks during the cancer treatment process.

There are so many things that can be said about this group of people. Words like teamwork, sacrifice, love, a common vision, togetherness and camaraderie just begin to touch the depth of this story. I am sure while you read this story words and pictures came to you as well.

The highest form of teamwork is the self-directed and managed team. It is obvious that this organization has a very special group of employees who have come together in this circumstance to perform at an extremely high level. The management team recognized the opportunity to be a part of a special moment. Hopefully, the management team will also recognize that this team is capable of much more than position or title would indicate.

This is a story that sounds good every day. In this holiday season, keep in mind

that your people and their teamwork are keys to your organization's success.
– December 6, 2009

30. Value Proposition

A value proposition, according to one definition, is an innovation or feature intended to make a company or product or service attractive to customers. In my experience, value propositions can also be applied to nonprofit organizations, government, educational and civic organizations. In my opinion, value proposition even extend to personal relationships.

A number of firms come to mind that have enhanced or changed their value propositions and in the process have changed the business landscape.

Amazon, in the beginning, was an online book seller. The impact of the new and efficient way of purchasing books was initially viewed as having a major impact primarily on the small and intermediate book stores. Fast forward to today and the expansion of Amazon into a full-fledged retail business, Amazon Prime subscription business and Amazon Web Services (AWS) is nothing short of amazing. Now, with the scope of services, innovation, logistical capabilities, financial strength and customer service, Amazon is poised to offer its value proposition in new and multiple ways.

Apple, at one time, was a personal computer company with a strong foothold in the academic and arts market segments. The value proposition offered by Apple changed the personal electronics landscape with Apple music and the various product replacements for what used to be the compact disc market. Apple has continued to offer new products and services based upon its technology, innovation and product design, and continues to change the market and our lives.

I have a friend who owns a Tesla Model X. When he refers to his vehicle the description includes the model year and vehicle's operating system release. Think about that for a moment.

The value propositions have continued with a marketing campaign for the Nissan Leaf, in one of the advertisements the voice-over states that "we provide technology that moves people". That statement is a clear change in the value proposition and potential relationship with their customers.

The above are just a few examples of how value propositions and organizational re-positioning are occurring in business at an increasing rate. It is not hard to see that if the value proposition you offer your customers is not renewed, with innovation, technology and other features, you could be in danger of becoming extinct.

On a personal level, think about how you have changed and the value proposition offered by your friendships. Golf is a good example. If you grew up playing golf, good for you. If you were introduced to the game in adulthood, you might find that some of your friends who did not make the transition to becoming golfers are not a part of your golfing life. For you, the value proposition of friendship has a new component, golf.

Your value proposition is more than a marketing campaign or slogan. I submit that it should be a cornerstone of your strategic planning and customer service strategy. To develop and maintain the relevance of your value proposition it will take time and effort. But, as we see in the above examples, getting your value proposition correct can be extremely successful. – May 27, 2018

31. The P (Rho) Organization

I n marketing concepts, there is the marketing mix, known as the "4 Ps," which represent *product, place, promotion and price* of a service or product.

I would like to present to you the Rho organization, which in its organizational structure also utilizes four Ps but with different meanings. The Rho organization utilizes the four P's to represent planning, projects, programs and process. The four Ps in a Rho organization describe the management and the cultural structure.

The letter P (Rho) is the 17th letter in the Greek alphabet. Also, in the system of Greek numerals, it has a value of 100.

At first glance, the model of a Rho organization is clear and relatively simple. The model starts with planning. It then moves to project, followed by programs and finally to processes.

Few would debate the necessity and value of planning for your organization or in your personal life. The key is that in a Rho organization, planning is a vigorous, continuous activity in which everyone in the organization has a role to play. More on that in a moment.

Project management, a key individual and organizational skill, follows from the planning module. I contend that project management is one of the best management techniques and is very easy to grasp for most of your team members. Additionally, an investment in understanding the terms and techniques of project management is transferable from one organization to another. Perhaps most important, project management instills a discipline throughout the organization that reduces over commitment.

The first time we do something, we utilize project management techniques. After the first project the next few attempts at that activity, depending on your business, fall into the program stage. Programs are based upon successful projects. Staff and resources are assigned to programs. Programs play the pivotal role between projects and processes. In the program stage there is significant learning and documentation of the activity to determine whether this is an activity that will become a part of the organization.

After a few cycles of the program and the decision to integrate it into the organization, the activity becomes a process. At the process level, the program team continues or transfers the knowledge of the program to those who then work to optimize the program by turning it into a process. At this time, process management disciplines are put in place to make the process replicable, definable, repeatable, scalable, measurable and efficient. The last step in a process is to report the outcomes of the process activity which can be direct input into the planning process.

The Rho organization has come full circle or can be considered a closed loop process. All members of the organization have input, based upon their level and involvement, into the planning for the next business cycle.

A Rho organization, by its design and discipline, addresses three significant management concerns: internal communications, staff capability and organizational culture. These concerns relate directly to an organization's ability to be nimble enough to react and seize market opportunities.

   – October 14, 2015

The P (Rho) Organization

Copyright The Parker Wright Group, Inc., 2015

About the Author

Cornell N. Wright is the principal of The Parker Wright Group, Inc., a training and management consulting practice, located in Stratford, CT, that specializes in management development, customer service, SWOT analysis, organizational assessments, strategy development and non-profit Board development.

Cornell N. Wright is a trainer, executive coach and management consultant with more than 40 years of business experience. He worked in the large corporate environment with IBM more than 19 years. While at IBM he worked with large, complex clients in systems, sales, marketing, management, and consulting capacities. Additionally, he has worked extensively with small to mid-sized companies in his own training and management consulting firm—The Parker Wright Group, Inc. established in 1994.

Cornell N. Wright has extensive management experience both practically and theoretically. He holds a Master of Business Administration from the University of Bridgeport, is a Certified Focus Group Director and he certified as a Practitioner in Inventory Management from the American Production and Inventory Control Society.

He is a member of the adjunct faculty at Housatonic Community College, Bridgeport, CT. He teaches courses in consumer behavior, organization management and customer service. In 2006, he was recognized in *Who's Who of American Teachers*. Since 2008, he has written a business column, "Plan Well and Execute" for the *New Haven Register*, New Haven, Connecticut.

In 2008, his firm was recognized as the *Small Business of the Year* by the Greater New Haven Chamber of Commerce.